THE SCOTTISH CLANS

and their

TARTANS

THE SCOTTISH CLANS

and their

TARTANS

with ninety-six color plates

**CHARTWELL
BOOKS, INC.**

00 22 3964 Q

Published by
CHARTWELL BOOKS, INC.
A Division of **BOOK SALES, INC.**
110 Enterprise Avenue
Secaucus, New Jersey 07094.

ISBN 1-55521-797-4

Printed and bound in Hong Kong.

929·3411

Contents

Introduction

THE SCOTTISH HIGHLANDERS are the remnant of the great Celtic race which remained untouched by the Roman and Saxon invasions on the south, and the incursions of Danes and Norsemen on the east and west of the country, and they were the last to oppose with perfect success the otherwise conquering armies of Rome. When, in 81AD, Agricola invaded North Britain, it was inhabited by twenty-one aboriginal tribes or clans.

The introduction of clanship and tartans seems to be beyond the reach of history, but Logan, in his *Scottish Gael*, gives the following extract from the charge and discharge of John, Bishop of Glasgow, Treasurer to King James III, 1471:

> *Ane elne and ane halve of Blue Tartane, to lyne*
> *his gowne of cloth of gold* . . . . £1, 10s.
> *Four elne and ane halve of Tartane, for a spartwort*
> *aboun his credill, price ane elne 10s* . . . . £2, 5s.
> *Halve ane elne of doble Tartane, to lyne ridin*
> *collars to her lady the Queen, price* . . . . *8 shillins.*

In the accounts of the Lord High Treasurer of Scotland, in August 1538, are entries regarding a Highland dress for King James V, on the occasion of that monarch making a hunting excursion to the Highlands. The dress was made of vari-coloured tartan.

In more modern times the following references may be quoted. In 1640, General Leslie states that the Highlanders under his command were composed of men of the same name or clan; as to the Tartan, reference is made to its price in the Acts of Parliament of Scotland in 1661. In the ornamental title to Bleau's Map of Scotland, published in 1654, two Highlanders are represented in striped cloths, one of them wearing the 'Belted Plaid,' consisting of a large and long piece of plaiding, which was so folded and confined by a belt round the waist as to form a complete dress, plaid and kilt in one piece.

Tartan is not a Gaelic word; the striped or spotted cloth under this name is called 'Breacan', derived from *breac*, chequered. Various coloured cloths have, from a very early period, been worn by the several Highland Clans, and originally tartan was worn only by the natives inhabiting the Highlands, which not only excluded the Lowlands or Border counties on the south, but also the north-east of the country. Later, however, many other tartans were invented and manufactured, and named after the Border tribes of the Lowlands, such as Douglas, Johnston, Lindsay, Dundas, etc. These, although not strictly considered Clan Tartans, are also described and illustrated in this book.

On the 1st day of August 1747 (O.S.), after the rising of 1745, an Act was passed forbidding the wearing of tartan, as any part of a Highland dress, under the penalty of six months' imprisonment for the first offence, and transportation overseas for seven years for the second.

No Highlander could receive the benefit of the Act of Indemnity without first taking the following dreadful oath:

'I, —, do swear, and as I shall answer to God at the great day of judgment, I have not, nor shall have, in my possession any gun, sword, pistol, or arm whatsoever, and never use tartan, plaid, or any part of the Highland garb; and if I do so, may I be cursed in my undertakings, family, and property; may I never see my wife and children, father, mother, or relations; may I be killed in battle as a coward, and lie without Christian burial, in a strange land, far from the graves of my forefathers and kindred; may all this come across me if I break my oath.'
Dr. James Browne's *History of the Highland Clans*, 1859.

This severe and harsh Act, as might have been expected, was most unpopular, and, in consequence of the discontent created by it, it was in 1782 repealed through the influence of the gallant Duke of Montrose.

When the last hope of the restoration of the Stewart dynasty was extinguished at Culloden (*'Culloden! which reeks with the blood of the brave'*), the influence of the Clans was greatly weakened, and by the making of military roads through the Highlands by General Wade, the face of the country and the habits of the people have been completely changed.

'Yet when time shall have drawn its veil over the past, as over the present, when the last broadsword shall have been broken on the anvil, and the shreds of the last plaid been tossed by the winds upon the cairn, or bleached within the raven's nest, posterity may look back with regret to a people who have so marked the history, the poetry, and the achievements of distant ages, and who, in the ranks of the British army, have stood foremost in the line of battle and given place to none'.

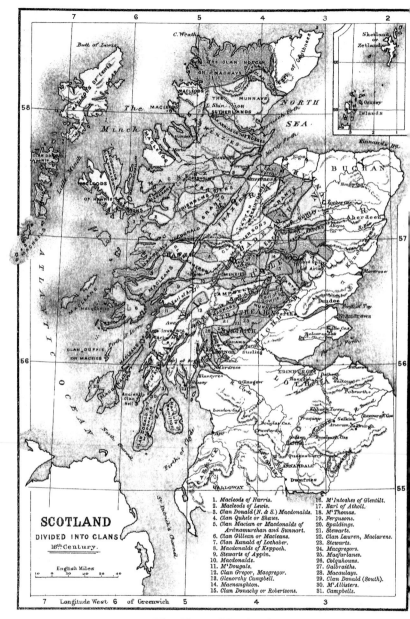

The Clans of Scotland

THE SCOTTISH
CLANS
and their
TARTANS

Brodie
of Brodie

BADGE: *Periwinkle.*
MOTTO: *Unite.*

THE CLAN Brodie is almost certainly of Pictish stock, and from the earliest times has been associated with Morayshire. The possession of land there was confirmed by Malcolm IV in 1160. Records of the family were lost in 1645 when Brodie house was burnt down by Lord Lewis Gordon, afterwards Marquis of Huntley.

Brodies have long been prominent in Scottish affairs, and Alexander Brodie (1617-1679) helped negotiate the return of Charles II. The family is connected through marriage to many great Scottish families. The seat of the chief is Brodie Castle in Morayshire.

1. BRODIE.

Bruce

BADGE: *Rosemary.*

MOTTO: *Fuimus (We have been)*

SIR ADAM DE BRUS (named after the town of Brix in Normandy) accompanied William the Conqueror to England. The connection with Scotland was established when his son Robert became companion in arms to Prince David, later David I. He received the Lordship of Annandale. The seventh Lord of Annandale became the famous Robert the Bruce, victor of Bannockburn. Bruce lands were enlarged by acquisitions in Clackmannanshire and Elgin. The Earls of Elgin are descended from the Bruce of Clackmannan.

2. BRUCE.

Buchanan

BADGE: *Bilberry, oak.*

MOTTO: *Clarior hinc honos (Brighter hence
the honour).*

WAR CRY: *Clar Innis! (An island on Loch
Lomond.)*

THE LANDS of Buchanan lie on the eastern shore
of Loch Lomond, from which it is thought that
the clan takes its name, though it may be derived
from the old Gaelic *Buth chanain*, son of the canon,
which indicates descent from one of the sacred
families of the old Celtic church. Sir Absolon of
Buchanan was granted the lands by the mighty
Earls of Lennox in the early 13th century. The lands
remained in the clan's possession until the death of
John, 22nd laird of Buchanan in 1682.

The clan supported Robert the Bruce in his
struggle for Scottish independence, and sent 7000
men to assist the French king after the Battle of
Agincourt in 1415. It is claimed that Sir Alexander
Buchanan killed the Duke of Clarence at the Battle
of Bauge in 1421. The chief of the clan fell at
Flodden in 1513.

3. BUCHANAN.

Cameron
of Erracht

BADGE: *Crowberry or oak.*
MOTTO: *Unite, for King and Country.*
WAR CRY: *Chlanna nan con thigibh a so's gheibh sibh feòil!*
PIPE MUSIC: *Pibroch of Donald Dubh.*

THE FIRST member of this family was Ewen, son of Ewen, thirteenth Chief of Lochiel by his second wife Marjory MacIntosh in the first half of the 16th century.

Donald Cameron, the second Laird of Erracht, joined Prince Charles Edward at the muster of the clans at Glenfinnan, as second in command of the Camerons under Cameron of Lochiel. His son, Sir Alan Cameron of Erracht, after a raffish start in life, served in America and was imprisoned in Philadelphia for two years, but on the outbreak of the Napoleonic war raised the 19th Regiment, the Cameron Highlanders.

Family lands were in Lochiel and northern Argyll.

4. CAMERON, ERRACHT.

Cameron
of Lochiel

BADGE: *Oak or Crowberry.*
MOTTO: *Unite, for King and Country.*
WAR CRY: *Chlanna nan con thigibh a so's gheibh sibh feòil!*
PIPE MUSIC: *The head of the high bridge, Pibroch of Donald Dubh.*

THE CAMERONS are reputed to be of the same origin as the Clan Chattan, but by the end of the 14th century there were three branches, the Camerons of Glenevis, of Strone and the MacMartins of Letterfinlay. The Lochiel Camerons descended from the Strone branch and their lands were Lochiel and northern Argyll.

The most notable member of the Clan was Sir Ewen Cameron (1629-1719), 'The Great Cameron' who is said to have killed the last wolf in Scotland and to have bitten out the throat of a Roundhead soldier. His grandson Donald, 'the Gentle Lochiel' was a staunch supporter of the Stuart cause and was one of the first to declare for Charles Edward at Glenfinnan in 1745.

5. CAMERON OF LOCHEIL.

Campbell of Argyll

BADGE: *Myrtle or Fir Club Moss.*
MOTTO: *Forget not.*
WAR CRY: *Cruachan!*
PIPE MUSIC: *The Campbells are coming,*
The Marquis lament.

THE CLAN CAMPBELL was for centuries the most powerful of the Scottish clans, rising on the ruins of the MacDonalds. Their policy was to 'supplant and ruin the race', and enmity between the two clans lasts to this day.

It is reputed that they are descended from Diamid, the Fingalian hero, who slew a venomous wild boar, and the family crest is a boar's head. Archibald, the first Marquis, always prominent in Scottish affairs, was beheaded in 1661, and his son Colin suffered the same fate in 1685 for supporting Monmouth's rebellion. His son Archibald supported William of Orange and was created the first Duke of Argyll in 1701. The present Dukes are descended from him.

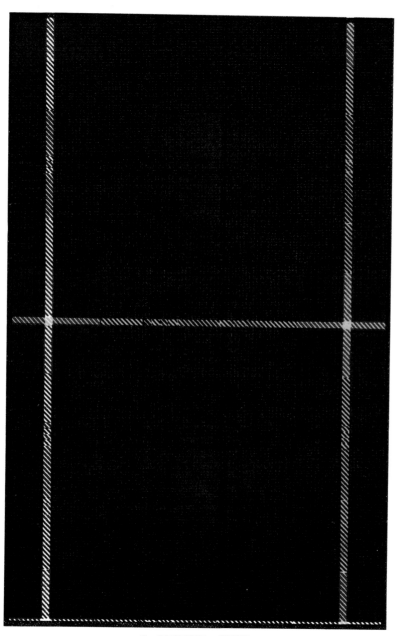

6. CAMPBELL, CHIEF.

Campbell of Breadalbane

BADGE: *Wild Myrtle or Fir Club Moss.*
MOTTO: *Follow me.*
WAR CRY: *Cry Cruachan!*
PIPE MUSIC: *The Carls with the breeks.*

THE CAMPBELLS of Breadalbane are a junior branch of the Campbells of Argyll, and are descended from Colin, a much travelled man who became a Knight Hospitaler of Rhodes. From his father he obtained the lands of Glenarchy, following the expulsion of the MacGregors.

The descendants of Sir Colin added to the family possessions including the lands of Glenlyon, Finlarig and territory throughout Argyll and Perthshire. Sir Colin Campbell was created first Earl of Breadalbane in 1681 and was a committed supported of Charles II. He was said to be destitute of all scruple, cunning as a fox, wise as a serpent and slippery as an eel. In 1689 he was employed to bribe the Highland clans to support William III.

7. CAMPBELL OF BREADALBANE.

Campbell of Cawdor

BADGE: *Bog Myrtle, Fir Club Moss.*
MOTTO: *Be Mindful.*
WAR CRY: *Cruachan!*
PIPE MUSIC: *Campbell of Cawdor's Salute.*

THE FIRST CAMPBELL of the Cawdor line was Sir John Campbell, third son of the second Earl of Argyll. He acquired the Cawdor estates through his wife Muriel. *The Book of the Thanes of Cawdor* describes him as a 'Campbell of the old stamp, seeking incessantly to increase his possessions and extend his influence'. Although members of the Cawdor family did not play dramatic roles in Scottish history they frequently served as members of Parliament, and were raised to the peerage first as Barons, and in 1827 as Earls. In the last 100 years the family has produced military heroes who have won no less than 16 Distinguished Service Orders and three Victoria Crosses. The present Earl still lives in Cawdor Castle.

8. CAMPBELL OF CAWDOR.

Campbell of Loudoun

BADGE: *Wild Myrtle, Fir Club Moss.*
MOTTO: *Byde my Time.*
WAR CRY: *Cruachan!*

THE FIRST of the present house of Loudoun was Sir Duncan Campbell, the ancestor of the Dukes of Argyll. Related on his mother's side to the great Sir William Wallace, he became Baron of Loudoun in 1381.

The family was raised to the Earldom of Loudoun by Charles I in 1633. Thereafter, male members of the family generally pursued military careers, Major-General James Campbell being killed at the battle of Fontenoy in 1745. The fourth Earl achieved the highest military honours and became Governor of Virginia and Edinburgh Castle, and was appointed Commander of the Forces in America in 1756 at the outbreak of the Seven Years War.

9. CAMPBELL OF LOUDOUN.

Chisholm

BADGE: *Alder or fern.*
MOTTO: *I am fierce with the fierce.*
PIPE MUSIC: *Chisholm's march.*
   Lament for William Chisholm.

IN OLD ENGLISH literature, Chisholm means 'a watermeadow good for producing cheese'. Probably of Anglo-Norman stock, the Chisholms flourished first in the Borders, but after the mid-fourteenth century and a fortunate marriage to the daughter of the Constable of Urquhart Castle on Loch Ness the family made its home in Inverness-shire.

One chief of the clan maintained that only three people might preface their title with the definite article – the Pope, the King and the Chisholm. The clan supported Prince Charles Edward valiantly, and a Chisholm was one of the seven men of Glenmoriston who aided the Prince during his escape to France after the Battle of Culloden in 1746.

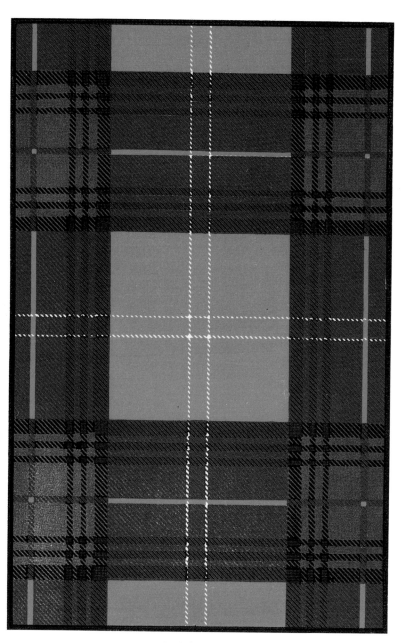

10 CHISHOLM.

The Clergy

BADGE: *The Burning Bush.*
MOTTO: *And it was not consumed.*

THE SCOTTISH CLERGY as a matter of custom often carried arms, especially when accompanying the Clan chieftain. About 200 years ago there is an attested account of a clerical MacLeod of Skye going to church with his two-handed sword, followed by a servant carrying his bow and case of arrows.

Many Highland names are of ecclesiastical origin, such as Clark, Gilchrist, Gillespie, Machilchrist, Mactaggart and McVicar.

11. CLERGY.

Colquhoun

BADGE: *Hazel or Dogberry.*
MOTTO: *If I can.*
WAR CRY: *Cnoc Ealachain!*
    (The clan's rallying place.)
PIPE MUSIC: *The Colquhoun March.*

THE CLAN COLQUHOUN is of Irish origin and the founder of the family was Henry de Kilpatrick who obtained a grant of lands by Loch Lomond from Malcolm, Earl of Lennox in the 13th century. Henry's successor Ingram was the first to assume the Colquhoun surname. In the following century Sir Robert Kilpatrick of Colquhoun married the daughter of the Laird of Luss since when the family has been described as of Colquhoun and Luss.

The motto is said to have come from Sir Iain Colquhoun who gave the reply 'Si je puis' when asked by James I of Scotland to recover Dumbarton Castle, in which he succeeded. The members of the family were distinguished servants of the crown. Perhaps the most memorable is Sir Humphrey Colquhoun, 16th of Luss, who in 1592 had an adulterous affair with the wife of the MacFarlane chief. Butchered by the MacFarlanes, he was served up in a dish to his former mistress.

12. COLQUHOUN

Cumin

BADGE: *Cumin plant*.
MOTTO: *Courage*.

THE CUMINS (also spelled Cumming or Comyn) first came to prominence during the reign of Malcolm Canmore in the 11th century. Opinion is divided as to whether the family came from Northumberland or Normandy (Commines). By the middle of the 13th century, the Cumins had become one of the mightiest families in Scotland, holding Badenoch as well as much of Lochaber and the Great Glen. They held three of thirteen Scottish Earldoms as well as the Constabulary of Scotland, and a Cumin endowed the rebuilding of Glasgow Cathedral.

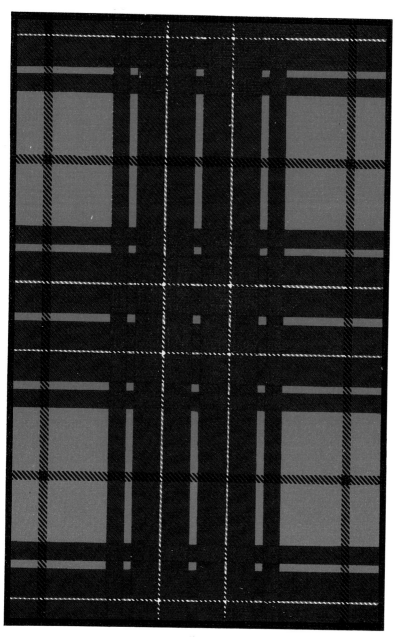

13. CUMIN.

Davidson

BADGE: *Red whortle berry.*
MOTTO: *Wisely if sincerely.*
PIPE MUSIC: *Tulloch's Salute,*
Tulloch Castle.

REPUTEDLY, the Davidsons are descended from David Dubh of Invernahavan, the first chief. His descendant Donald Dubh married into the Clan Mackintosh and sought protection of the Clan Chattan, the ancient federation of clans which encompassed the Mackintoshes, the Macphersons the MacGillivrays and the McBeans.

Never in the forefront of Scottish political affairs, the Davidsons flourished nonetheless. In the 18th century a branch of the Davidsons acquired the lands and castle of Tulloch in Ross-shire and became hereditary keepers of the Royal Castle of Dingwall.

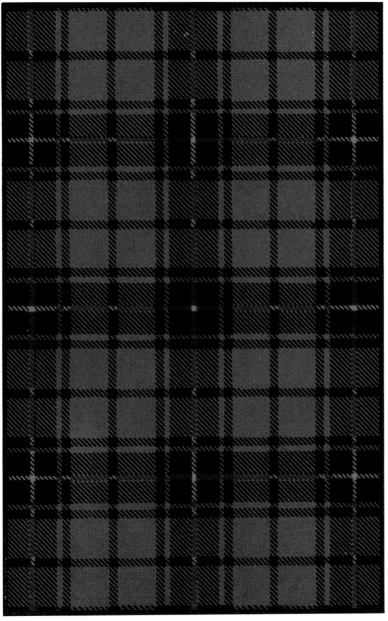

14.   DAVIDSON.

Douglas

BADGE: *A salamander, on a hat ablaze.*
MOTTO: *Never behind (Jamais arriere).*
WAR CRY: *A Douglas, a Douglas!*

THIS POWERFUL family seems to have risen to prominence in Lanarkshire in the 12th Century. The original family – the Black Douglases – wielded their influence in Lanark, Galloway and Dumfrieshire, while the junior branch, the Red Douglases, used their influence in lands to the east in Dalkeith and then Angus.

The family is closely linked to the Scottish throne. Sir James Douglas, known as 'The good Sir James', was one of Robert the Bruce's greatest captains, and was killed by the Moors in Spain on a journey to take King Robert's heart to Jerusalem for burial.

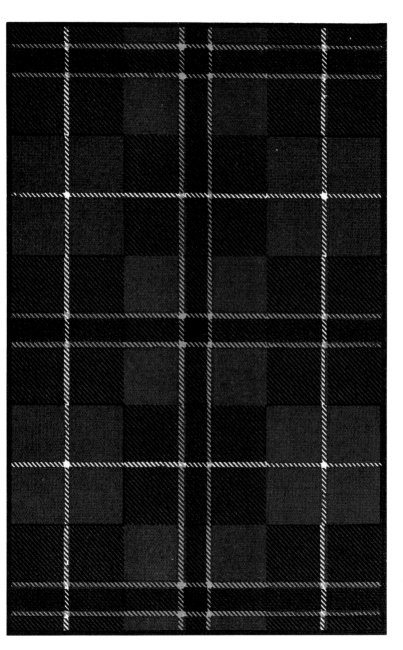

15.   DOUGLAS.

Drummond

BADGE: *Wild thyme or holly.*
MOTTO: *Gang warily.*
PIPE MUSIC: *Duke of Perth's March.*

THE DRUMMONDS are said to be descended from Maurice, Prince of Hungary, who had escorted Malcolm Canmore's bride-to-be to Scotland. He was granted the lands of Drummond or Drymen in Stirlingshire.

Sir Malcolm de Drymen fought with Bruce at Bannockburn and is credited with strewing the battlefield with spiked caltrops which took a massive toll of the English cavalry. Ever faithful to the Scottish crown and the Stuart cause, the Drummond estates were forfeited after the 1745 uprising.

16. DRUMMOND.

Dundas

SERLE DE DUNDAS was living in the time of King William the Lion (1143-1214). This prolific lowland family did not come to the fore in public affairs until the late 17th century when Sir James Dundas, Lord Arniston, became a Lord of Session. His descendants numbered many notable lawyers, including Henry Dundas (1742-1811) who was a strong supporter of William Pitt the younger, and became, among other things, Secretary for war and Home Secretary. Raised to peerage in 1802, he was impeached in 1806 for gross malversation while Secretary of the Navy.

17. DUNDAS.

Elliot

BADGE: *Armour-clad arm brandishing broad sword.*

MOTTO: *Fortiter et recte (With strength and right).*

THE ELLIOTS were a warlike border clan, but like the Dundases did not achieve political significance until the 17th and 18th centuries. George Elliot (1717-1790) was Governor of Gibraltar during its heroic defence from 1779 to 1783. He was created Lord Heathfield in 1787. Gilbert Elliot (1751-1814) of Stobs was an eminent Governor-General of India (1807-1812) and was created Earl of Minto in 1813.

18. ELLIOT.

Erskine

BADGE: *Hand holding a dagger out of a cap of maintenance.*

MOTTO: *Je pense plus (I think more).*

THE BARONY of Erskine in Renfrewshire was held by Sir Henry de Eskine in the 13th century. His descendants were prominent courtiers, and Sir Robert Erskine was Chamberlain of Scotland (1350-57). The family was prominent in the French Scots guards and fought under the leadership of Joan of Arc. The family acquired the Earldom of Buchan, and Thomas Erskine, third son of the 10th Earl, became Lord Chancellor of England in 1806.

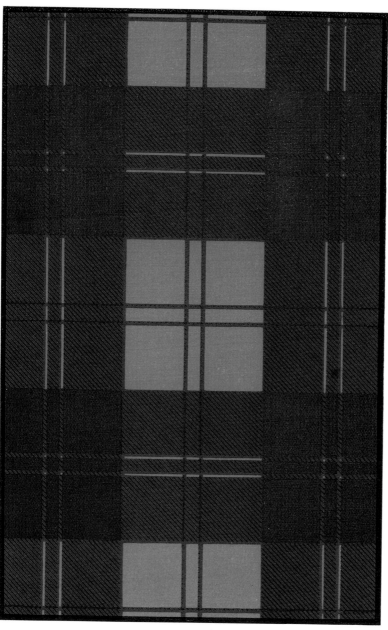

19. ERSKINE.

Farquharson

BADGE: *Whortleberry, Scotch fir, Foxglove.*

MOTTO: *Fide et fortitudine*
   (By fidelity and fortitude).

WAR CRY: *Carn na cuimhne!*

THE FARQUHARSON is an Aberdeenshire clan and was a member of the Clan Chattan. It takes its name from Farquhar, son of Shaw of Rothiemurchus who was forester to the Stewart Earl of Mar (c.1440).

Finlay Mor, a Farquharson, was Scottish Standard Bearer at the Battle of Pinkie (1547) where he was killed. The clan supported the Jacobite cause fighting bravely, but ineffectually, at both the battle of Preston in 1715 and Culloden in 1746.

20. FARQUHARSON.

Fergusson

BADGE: *Pine, poplar.*

MOTTO:*Dulcius ex asperis*
(Sweeter after difficulties).

THIS OLD and dispersed clan held lands in Argyll, Perthshire, Dunfries, Galloway and the estate of Raith. Distinguished members of the family include Robert Fergusson (1637-1714) known as 'the Plotter' for his treasonable schemes against the last two Stuart Kings, and Adam Fergusson the philosopher, historian and close friend of Sir Walter Scott.

Since the 18th century the Fergussons have been notable public servants and soldiers, the most recent being Sir Bernard Fergusson, who fought with distinction as a Chindit in Burma, and who followed his father and both his grandfathers as Governor-General of New Zealand.

21. FERGUSSON.

Forbes

BADGE: *Broom.*
MOTTO: *Grace me guide.*
WAR CRY: *Lonach! (A mountain in Strathdon.)*
PIPE MUSIC: *The Battle of Glen Eurann.*

THIS DISTINGUISHED family became one of the most powerful in the north-east of Scotland. Descended from John Forbes of Forbes, the family has held lands on Don-side since the 13th century.

Of pragmatic tradition, the Forbes clan struggled long for supremacy against the Gordons, supporters of the 'Old Faith', and Mary, Queen of Scots. As Covenanters and Whigs, the Forbes family supported the Hanoverian Succession, Duncan Forbes of Culloden using his influence as Lord President of the Court of Sessions to prevent many clans joining Charles Edward in 1745.

22. FORBES

The Black Watch

BADGE: *St Andrew's Cross on Star of the Order of the Thistle.*

MOTTO: *Nemo me impune lacessit (No-one attacks me with impunity).*

THE ORIGINS of this distinguished regiment go back to 1729 when the Government raised six companies of Highlanders (three each of 100 men, three each of 75) to keep the peace. Ten years later it was decided to increase the number to 1000.

Until 1739 each company was dressed in tartan chosen by its commander, but, as the companies were now to form a regiment, a uniform tartan was necessary. The first Colonel, Lord Crawford, had made the distinctive dark tartan which so contrasted with the scarlet uniforms of the regular army that the regiment was called the Black Watch.

23. FORTY-SECOND, "BLACK WATCH," AND CLAN CAMPBELL.

Fraser

BADGE: *Yew.*

MOTTO: *Je suis prest (I am ready).*

WAR CRY: *A Mhor-fhaiche!*
Caistel Dunie!

PIPE MUSIC: *Lovat's Lament.*

THE FRASERS are not of Gaelic descent, though the family has been settled in Scotland for many years – some say from Pierre Fraser who arrived in Scotland in 790 AD. Their lands were originally in East Lothian, but later in Aberdeenshire, where Sir Alexander Fraser (1537-1623) founded the port of Fraserburgh.

In medieval times perhaps the most distinguished member of the family was Sir Simon Fraser who sided with William Wallace, defeated the English three times in one day at the battle of Rosslyn in 1302, and was captured when fighting for Robert the Bruce. Edward I commanded that he be put to death, and he was hanged, drawn and quartered. The family acquired the baronry of Lovat, but the part played by Lord Lovat, 'the Old Fox', in the '45 rebellion caused it to be attainted. The title was revived in the 19th century.

24. FRASER.

Gordon

BADGE: *Ivy*.

MOTTO: *Bydand (Remaining)*.

WAR CRY: *A Gordon, a Gordon!*

PIPE MUSIC: *The Gordon's March*.

THE GORDONS are an Anglo-Norman family who settled in Berwickshire in the 11th century. In the 14th century they were granted lands in Aberdeenshire, where their prominence caused the chief to be known as 'Cock of the North'.

The clan gave birth to many distinguished offspring. Adam de Gordon who fought in the 1270 crusade with Louis XII of France, Lord George Gordon, the disreputable Georgian agitator, of Gordon Riots fame, George Gordon Lord Byron and 'Chinese' Gordon who was killed at Khartoum. The Gordon Highlanders were raised in 1794 with the assistance of Jane, Duchess of Gordon.

25. GORDON.

Graham

BADGE: *Laurel.*
MOTTO: *Ne oublie (Do not forget).*
PIPE MUSIC: *Killiecrankie,*
Claverhouse Lament.

ALTHOUGH ANCIENT tradition has it that the Grahams are descended from Grammus, a famous warrior who breached the Roman Wall in AD 420 winning for it the nickname Graham's Dyke, in fact the family is almost certainly of Anglo-Norman descent. The first recorded mention of the name is that of Sir William de Graham who witnessed the charter of the Abbey of Holyrood in 1128 and was granted lands in Abercorn and Dalkeith by King David I.

The Grahams fought valiantly for both Wallace and Bruce in the 14th century wars of independence, and supported the Stuarts in the 17th century. James Graham (1612-50) first Marquis Montrose, a romantic Royalist general, was executed in 1650, and a kinsman, John Graham of Claverhouse, Viscount Dundee (1649-89) known as 'Bonnie Dundee' or 'Bloody Clavers' depending on allegiance, who was killed in his hour of triumph against the Covenanters at the Battle of Killiecrankie.

26. GRAHAM

Grant

BADGE: *Pine.*
MOTTO: *Stand fast.*
WAR CRY: *Creag Elachaidh.*

THERE ARE SEVERAL traditions about the origin of the Clan Grant. One claims that the Grants are descended from Kenneth MacAlpine, High King of Picts and Scots (died AD 860) and another that they are of Norman descent (their name being simply a Norman nickname Le Grand, meaning big) acquiring lands in Scotland by marrying into the Bissets of Invernesshire. Traditionally, the Grants have held lands in Strathspey, Rothiemurchus, Glenmoriston and Loch Ness.

Patrick Grant of Crasky was one of the seven men of Glenmopriston who sheltered Charles Edward Stuart after Culloden, and eighty-four of his kinsman who laid down their arms in May 1746 were transported to Barbnados in violation of their terms of surrender and sold as slaves. Sir Ludovic Grant of Grant (1743-73) was the founder and designer of Grantown-on-Spey.

27. GRANT.

Gunn

BADGE: *Juniper or Roseroot.*
MOTTO: *Aut pax aut bellum*
    (Either peace or war).
PIPE MUSIC: *The Gunn's Salute.*

THIS WARLIKE and ferocious family emerged as a clan in the 13th century after Gunn, said to be the son of Olave the Black, Norse king of Man and the Isles, obtained Caithness through marriage to Ragnhild, heiress of Harold Ugni, Earl in Orkney and Earl in Caithness.

Continual feuding with other clans, notably the Keiths, the Mackays and the Earls of Caithness and Sutherland which involved raids, betrayals and the abduction of a Gunn heiress, ended in eventual defeat for the Gunns and most of the clan emigrated to Sutherland.

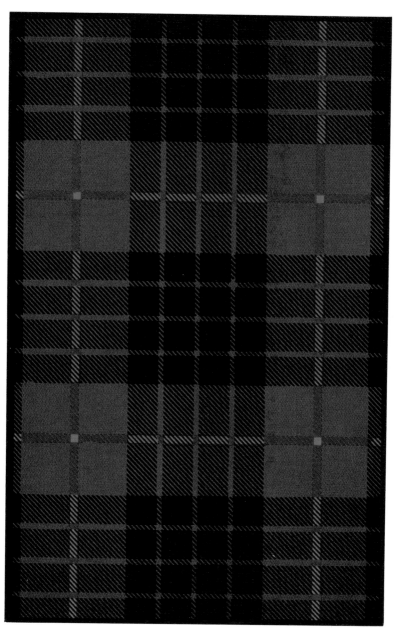

28. GUNN.

The Jacobite Tartan

THIS TARTAN, one pattern of which is shown here, was worn as one of the emblems of the Jacobites before and during the 1715 uprising.

It was one of many secret signs and emblems, and doubtless it was adopted as a symbol to others of secret political opinions, like the S (for Stuart) in the open-work of the hilt of the Claymore, or the legend *No union* on its blade.

29. JACOBITE.

Johnston

BADGE: *Red hawthorn.*
MOTTO: *Nunquan non paratus*
(Never unprepared).

THE JOHNSTONS were a powerful and warlike clan who derived their name from the barony of Johnston in Annandale. They were prominent in Border warfare from the 13th century and were loyal supporters of the crown.

The northern Johnstons claim descent from Stiven de Johnston who possessed lands of Ballindalloch, and George Johnstone of that ilk was created a Baron of Nova Scotia in 1626. Sir John Johnston, the 3rd Baronet, was executed in 1690 for supposedly taking part in the abduction of an heiress.

30. JOHNSTON.

Kerr

BADGE: *The sun in splendour.*

MOTTO: *Sero sed serio*
(Late but in earnest).

THE KERRS were an Anglo-Norman family first found in Scotland at the end of the 12th century. They were prominent in border warfare, and the Kerrs of Cessford were Wardens of the Marches, and were granted old Roxburghe by James IV. This branch gained the lordship in 1600, and for supporting the Act of Union in 1707 the dukedom in 1708.

31. KERR.

Lamond or Lamont

BADGE: *Crab apple.*

MOTTO: *Ne parcas nec spernas*
(Neither spare nor dispose).

THE LAMONTS take their name from Ladmon, a chief who was living in Cowall in 1238. He belonged to the dynastic family of Cowall and Knapdale, and was descended from the Irish prince Anrothan (Son of Aodh O'Neill, king of the North of Ireland 1030-1033) who had crossed the sea to Argyll and married the daughter of a local king.

The Clan Lamont, once the greatest power in Cowall, was much diminished by the encroachment of the Campbells. In 1646, the Campbells burnt the Lamont Castles of Toward and Ascog, and treacherously murdered over 200 of the clan, putting women and children to the sword, and half-hanging, then burying alive the men.

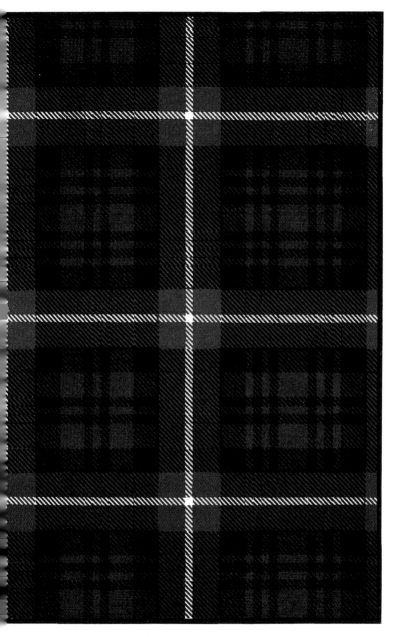

32.   LAMOND.

Leslie

BADGE: *Rue*.
MOTTO: *Grip fast*.

THE BARONY of Leslie is in Aberdeenshire, and the first recorded proprietor is Bartholf de Leslie during the reign of William the Lion (1165-1214). George Leslie of Rothes was raised to the peerage in 1457 as Earl of Rothes and Lord Leslie.

General Alexander Leslie of Balgonie served under Gustavus Adolphus in the Thirty Years War and rose to become Field-Marshall. Invited back to Scotland to command the Covenanters, he captured Edinburgh Castle with 1000 men. In spite of being created Earl of Leven by Charles I, he led an army into England and took part in the defeat of the King at Marston Moor in 1644. His nephew David served under him and commanded the Scottish Royalists at the battle of Dunbar. He was created Baron Newark after the Restoration.

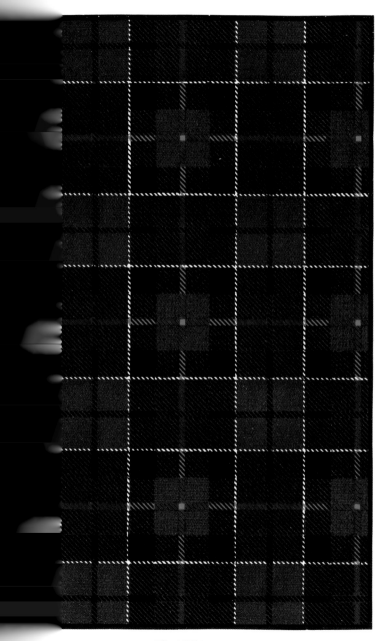

33. LESLIE.

Lindsay

BADGE: *Rue, lime tree.*
MOTTO: *Endure fort (Endure with strength).*

THOUGH THERE IS a tradition that the Lindsays are descended through Randolph, Sire de Toeny from Ivar, Jarl of the Uplanders, they were originally Anglo-Norman barons holding lands in Normandy and England towards the end of the 11th century. The family acquired lands in Lanarkshire, and Sir David Lindsay of Glenesk was created Earl of Crawford in 1398. He married a daughter of Robert II, and as a part of the dowry received the Barony of Strathnairn in Invernesshire.

The centuries-old holdings of the Lindsays in the highlands have long since been lost, but the family still flourishes. Its chief is the Earl of Crawford and Balcarres.

34. LINDSAY.

Logan or MacLennan

BADGE: *Furze*.

MOTTO: *Hoc majorum virtus (This is the valour of my ancestors)*.

WAR CRY: *Druim-nan-deur!*

THE LOGANS consist of Lowland and Highland families. The southern Logans originated in Logan in the Lothians, whereas the Logans of the North, the Siol Ghillinnein, the MacLennans, are descended from the Logans of Drumderfit in Easter Ross.

The principal branch, the Logans of Restalrig, is now extinct, but the northern Logans flourish and the name MacLennan is still common in Ross-shire.

35. LOGAN or MACLENNAN.

MacAlister

BADGE: *Heath*.
MOTTO: *Fortiter (Boldly)*.

A LISTER (the Gaelic form of Alexander) was the younger son of Donald of Islay, Lord of the Isles and great-grandson of the famous Somerled. The clan is thereby related to the powerful Clan Donald.

The principal lands of this clan were in Kintyre, with holdings in Arran and Bute as well. An important branch of the family was the MacAlisters of Tarbert who under the Earls of Argyll were Constables of Tarbert Castle on Loch Fyne.

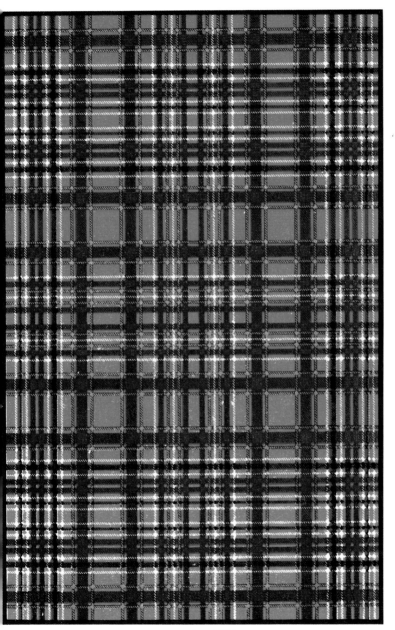

36. MACALISTER.

MacAlpine

BADGE: *Pine.*

MOTTO AND WAR CRY:
Cuimhnich bàs Ailpein.

ACCORDING to some records, the MacAlpines are descended from those venerable sons of antiquity whose successors became Kings of the Scots during 25 generations. The clan claims descent from King Alpin of the South who was murdered by the Pictish Brudas after the Battle of Dundee in AD834.

The Clan MacAlpine is landless, though the traditional home is Dunstaffnage in Argyll. It is a clan which is said to include the Grants, the MacGregors, MacKinnons, MacQuarries, MacNabs, MacDuffs and the MacAulays.

37. MACALPINE.

MacArthur

BADGE: *White myrtle or Fir-club moss.*
MOTTO: *Fide et opera*
    (By fidelity and work).
WAR CRY: *Eisd O'Eisd!*

THE MACARTHURS formed the senior branch of the Clan Campbell, and held the chiefdom until the 15th century. Some say that by remote descent they can claim the hero-king Arthur, son of Uther Pendragon, as a forbear, another tradition holds that they gained their name from Arthur Campbell who received Strachur from Robert II in the late 14th century. There is a saying that 'there is nothing older unless it be the hills, MacArthur or the Devil'.

The MacArthurs were strong supporters of Robert the Bruce, but lost their power in 1427 when John, the chief, was executed by James I. John MacArthur (b.1767), the 'Father of New South Wales', was commandant at Parramatta from 1793-1804 and took great interest in the development of the colony. He is credited with being the founder of the wool and wine industries there.

38. MACARTHUR.

MacAulay

BADGE: *Cranberry or Scottish fir.*
MOTTO: *Dulce Periculum*
  (Danger is sweet).

MACAULAY can mean 'son of Olaf' or 'son of Amalghaidh' – the former clan being of Norse, the latter of Gaelic origin. The Norse branch spring from Ullapool ('Olaf's place') on the mainland of Ross, and became the MacAulays of Lewis, which was a part of Norway until 1266. The historian, Thomas Babington, Lord MacAulay belonged to this branch.

The Gaelic MacAulays claimed descent from the Royal House of Munster, and membership through Aulay, brother of the Earl of Lennon, to the clan MacAlpine. Their lands were principally in Dunbartonshire, and they held Ardencaple Castle until 1767 when it was sold to the Duke of Argyll.

39. MACAULAY.

MacBean

BADGE: *Box red whortleberry.*
MOTTO: *Touch not the catt bot a targe.*

THIS FIERCE and ancient clan are said to have come from Lochaber, originally descended from Donald Ban or Donalbane. He was the second son of Duncan I (who was succeeded by MacBeth). Tradition ranks the clan as one of the many tribes comprehended under the generic appellation of Clan Chattan.

Although a division of MacBeans fought under Lochiel in 1745, they generally ranked under the Mackintosh banner. Two heroes of the clan were Gillies MacBean who killed over a dozen dragoons defending a breach in a wall at the Battle of Culloden, and Major-General William MacBean who won a Victoria Cross in 1858 at the seige of Lucknow during the Indian Mutiny.

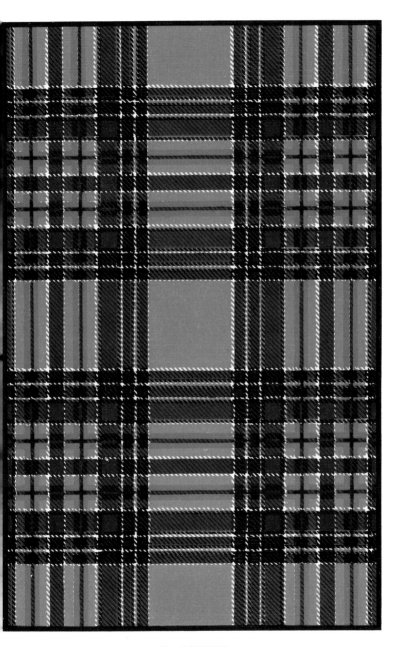

40 MACBEAN.

MacBeth

THIS OLD GAELIC clan held lands in Morayshire and Perthshire. Finlegh, Thane of Moray, was the father of King MacBeth (1040-57). Unlike Shakespeare's character, the historical MacBeth, the last truly Gaelic King of Scots, was a generous, wise and devout ruler, and he made a pilgrimage to Rome in 1050. He was killed at the Battle of Lumphanan, and buried in Iona, for many years the last resting place of Scottish Kings.

Other branches of the clan include the Beatons and the Bethunes.

41. MACBETH.

MacDonald

BADGE: *Heath.*

MOTTO: *Per mare per terras*
    (By sea and by land).

WAR CRY: *Fraoch Eilean!*

PIPE MUSIC: *March of the MacDonalds.*

THE CLAN MACDONALD was for centuries the mightiest of all highland clans. The surname is derived from Donald of Islay, Lord of the Isles (1162-1207), himself the grandson of the great Somerled. His son, Angus Og, supported Robert the Bruce and received grants of lands, and his grandson married into the Earldom of Ross. The MacDonalds feuded constantly with the monarchs of Scotland, and the lordship forfeited to the crown in 1493 is now among the titles of the Prince of Wales. After this, the name MacDonald was used as the surname of the clan. The MacDonalds of Glencoe, a sept or division of the clan, were faithful to the Stuart cause, and several were treacherously murdered by the troops of William of Orange in 1692.

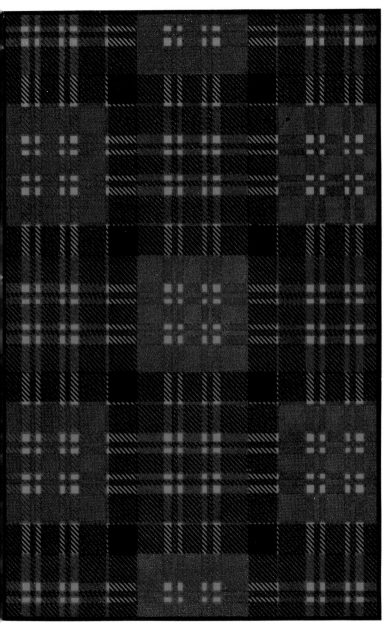

42. MACDONALD.

MacDonald of Clanranald

BADGE: *Heath*.

MOTTO: *My hope is constant in thee*.

WAR CRY: *Dh' aindeoin co theireadh e!*

PIPE MUSIC: *Clan Ranald's March, Clan Ranald's lament*.

T HE CLAN MACDONALD of Clanranald are descended from Ranald, the younger son of John MacDonald grandson of Angus Og. He received a grant of the North Isles and other lands in 1373. From him are descended the families of Moidart, Morar, Knoidart and Glengarry.

Flora MacDonald (1722-90) of South Uist was instrumental in conducting Charles Edward Stuart, disguised as a maidservant, to safety in Skye in 1746.

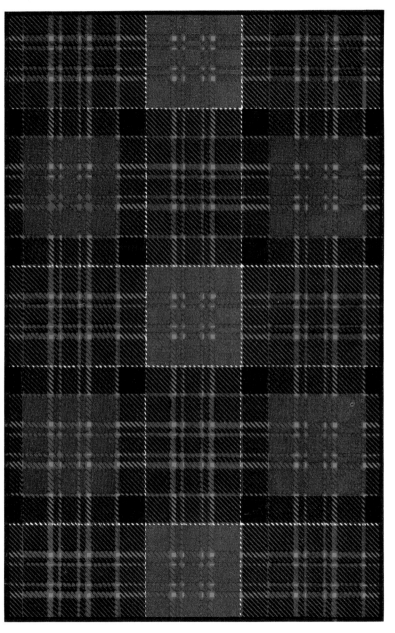

43. MACDONALD OF CLANRANALD.

MacDonnell of Glengarry

BADGE: *Heath.*

MOTTO: *Creag an Fhitich*
(The raven's rock).

WAR CRY: *Creag an Fhitich!*

PIPE MUSIC: *Glengarry's lament.*

THE MACDONNELS trace their descent from Donald, the son of Ronald the progenitor of the Macdonalds of Clanranald. Donald and his brothers were dispossessed of their Glengarry lands by their uncle, Godfrey. His son Alexander was executed in 1427 and the lands reverted to the Crown. The MacDonnells were thereafter Crown tenants.

600 Glengarry MacDonnells joined Charles Edward in 1745 under the chief's second son Angus. He and his father were imprisoned for a time in the Tower of London.

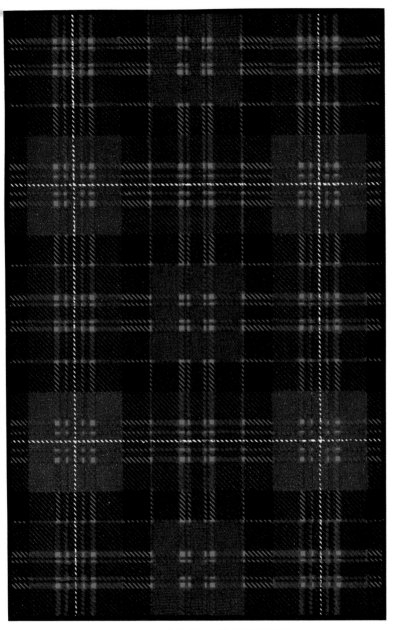

44. MACDONELL OF GLENGARRY.

MacDonald of the Isles and Sleat

BADGE: *Heath.*

MOTTO: *Per mare et per terras*
(By sea and by land).

ALL THE MACDONALDS were descended from Sumerled, King of the Isles, who drove out the Norsemen from the Western Isles. He was killed at the Battle of Renfrew in 1164 when fighting against Malcolm V, King of Scots.

The MacDonalds of the Isles are descended from the branch of the family that married into the Earldom of Ross. Those of Sleat are descended from Hugh, younger son of Alexander Macdonald, Earl of Ross and Lord of the Isles.

45. MACDONALD OF SLEAT.

MacDonald of Staffa

BADGE: *Heath.*

MOTTO: *Per mare et per terras*
(By sea and by land).

WAR CRY: *The heather Isle!*

THIS RELATIVELY modern family is descended from the MacDonalds of Benbecula and South Uist.

46. MACDONALD OF STAFFA.

MacDougall

BADGE: *Bell heath.*
MOTTO: *Victory or death.*
WAR CRY: *Buaidh no bas!*
PIPE MUSIC: *Dunolly Castle.*

THE MACDOUGALLS take their name from Dugall, eldest son of Somerled king of the Isles. After his father's death at Renfrew in 1164, he inherited Argyll and Lorn, together with Mull, Lismore, Kerrera, Scarba, Jura, Tiree and Coll. His sons were all three of them recognized as kings in 'the west beyond the sea', the southern Hebrides, by the High king of Norway. The MacDougal seat, Dunollie Castle in Oban bay, is of the same style and dimensions as the former castle of Bergen in Norway.

In 1273, Ewen MacDougall, king of Lorn and the South Isles submitted to the Crown. The clan came out for the Jacobite cause in 1715 and forfeited its lands, but these were restored after siding with the House of Hanover in 1745. The eldest daughter of the chief bears the old title 'the Maid of Lorn'.

47. MACDOUGAL.

MacDuff

BADGE: *Boxwood, Redwhortle*.
MOTTO: *Deus jurat (God assists)*.
PIPE MUSIC: *MacDuff's Lament*.

THE ORIGIN of this clan is clouded by fable. The first two known chiefs, the brothers Constantine and Gilmichael MacDuff, were successive Earls of Fife in the second quarter of the 12th century. No historical link with Shakespeare's MacDuff has been proved. The Earls of Fife were hereditary crown-bearers to the King of Scots, and the premier clan among the Gaels of medieval Scotland.

In more recent times, Alexander Duff (1849-1912), Duke of Fife and Earl of MacDuff, married Princess Louise, daughter of King Edward VII.

48. MACDUFF.

MacFarlane

BADGE: *Cranberry, Cloudberry.*
MOTTO: *This I'll defend.*
WAR CRY: *Loch Sloidh!*
PIPE MUSIC: *Lifting the cattle.*

THIS CLAN and surname are descended from the ancient Celtic Earls of the district to which they belonged – the Lennox in the western shire of Loch Lomond. Bartholomew or Parlan was the grandson of Gilchrist, 3rd Earl of Lennox.

This warlike and predatory clan was proscribed in the 16th and 17th centuries, deprived of its lands and name, and largely dispersed.

49. MACFARLANE.

MacFie

BADGE: *Pine, Oak.*
MOTTO: *Pro Rege (For the king).*

THE MACFIES are said to be a branch of the race of Alpine, and probably descend through the MacDuffs from Dubhsith (the Gaelic version) who was a Lector at the cathedral on Iona in the 12th century.

The chiefs of the clan, which was most numerous on Colonsay, adhered to the Lords of the Isles and, after their downfall, to the MacDonalds of Islay. In the 17th century Colonsay passed to the Campbells, and the family is now represented in the island by crofters.

50. MACFIE.

MacGillivray

BADGE: *Rosewood.*

MOTTO: *Dunmaglas.*

ORIGINALLY from the west, Morven and Lochaber, Clan MacGillivray was driven east to
Strathnairn in the 13th century by Alexander III. It
is one of the oldest branches of the Clan Chattan
confederation. However, a branch survived on the
island of Mull.

The clan was strong in the Jacobite cause and
McGillivray of Dunnaglas led the Clan Chattan at
the Battle of Culloden. It is recorded that an
Alexander MacGillivray became a Red Indian chief
in 1777.

51. MACGILLIVRAY.

MacGregor

BADGE: *Pine.*
MOTTO: *Royal is my race.*
WAR CRY: *Ard-Coille!*
PIPE MUSIC: *Chase of Glen Fruin.*

THE MACGREGORS claim descent from Griogar, the son of King Alpine, and their original lands of Glenorchy, Glenstrae, Glenlyon and Glengyle straddle the borders of Argyll and western Perthshire. In 1519, the Campbells managed to establish as chief of the whole Clan Gregor their own nominee, the MacGregor chieftain of a junior branch who had ravished, then married, Campbell of Glenorchy's daughter. The disinherited line resisted this takeover by brigandage and general lawlessness, so that in 1603 the clan Gregor was outlawed and the name of MacGregor proscribed on pain of death. It was repealed in 1774.

The Clan has a justified reputation for turbulence, numbering among its members not only Rob Roy MacGregor (1617-1734) a freebooter romanticized by Sir Walter Scott, but at least 22 who were hanged, four beheaded, three murdered and a chieftain who was scalped by American Indians in the mid 17th century.

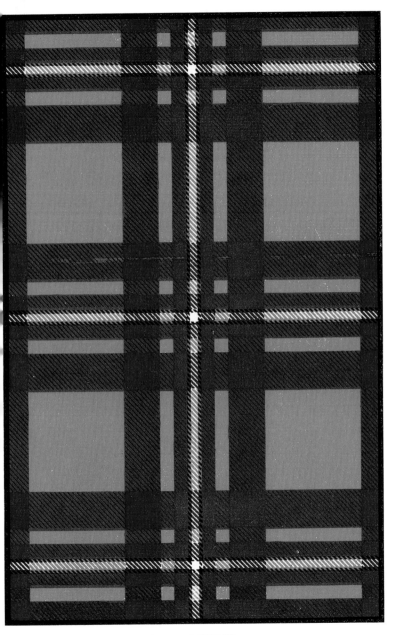

52. MACGREGOR.

Mackintosh or Macintosh

BADGE: *Box or redwhortle.*
MOTTO: *Touch not the cat bot a glove.*
WAR CRY: *Loch Moidheidh.*
PIPE MUSIC: *The Macintosh's Lament.*

THE MACINTOSH tradition is that their ancestor was a cadet of the clan McDuff of Fife, who married the heiress of the ancient captains of Clan Chattan in the early 12th century. The chief still quarters the red lion in gold of the MacDuffs on his shield and his standard.

The rise of the Macintoshes caused friction with other clans, and they joined the Covenanters rather than the King in 1639, though they opposed Cromwell in 1650. They were prominent in the Jacobite rising of 1715, and in supporting Prince Charles Edward in 1745. In the following year the Prince was the guest of Anne, Lady Macintosh at Moy, and half-a-dozen of her servants put to flight the 1500 government troops who had been sent to capture him – the Rout of Moy. Leading figures in more modern times include Charles Macintosh (1766-1843) inventor of the waterproof coat that bears his name, and the architect Charles Rennie Macintosh (1868-1928).

53. MACINTOSH.

Chief Macintosh

BADGE: *Box or red whortleberry.*
MOTTO: *Touch not the cat bot a glove.*

THIS TARTAN is supposed to be the genuine sett which has been worn by the chiefs of this distinguished clan for many generations. The chiefs of some clans wore separate tartans from their men, which accounts for there being two tartans for the name Macintosh.

54. MACINTOSH, CHIEF.

MacInnes

BADGE: *Holly.*

MOTTO: *Through the grace of God and the King.*

MORVEN, the district of Argyllshire celebrated in the poems of Ossian as the territory of the great Fingal, was the chief seat of the MacInnes clan. Certainly, it can claim descent from the ancient Celtic clan of Aongas or Angus.

The clan McInnes remained in possession of Morven until Montrose's general Coll Kitto defeated them and drove them away in 1645. After dispersal, some went to Skye and some joined the Campbells in Craignish.

55. MACINNES.

MacIntyre

BADGE: *Heath*.
MOTTO: *Per ardua (Through difficulties)*.
WAR CRY: *Cruachan!*
PIPE MUSIC: *We will take the highway*.

MACINTYRE derives from *Mac-an-t-saoir*, the Gaelic for 'son of a carpenter'. The father of the clan is said to have acquired his name while on a MacDonald galley, and who cut off his thumb to plug a leak in the ship. The clan has a close association with the clan Donald.

The principal family possessed the lands of Glenoe on Loch Etive, and were hereditary foresters to the Stewarts of Lorn. A family of MacIntyres were hereditary pipers to the chiefs of MacDonald of Clanranald, and another to the chiefs of clan Menzies. Members of the clan resident in Cladich were famous for their weaving of hose and garters.

56. MACINTYRE.

MacKay

BADGE: *Bulrush or broom.*
MOTTO: *Manu forti (With strong hands).*
WAR CRY: *Bratach bhan Chlann Aoidh!*
PIPE MUSIC: *MacKay's March, Lament of Donald MacKay.*

THE MACKAYS are descended from the royal house of Moray and were originally known as the clan Morgan. Morgan's grandson Aoidh gave them their present name. Their traditional lands were in Moray, but many of the clan were transported north by Malcolm IV in the 12th century. By the end of the 13th century, they controlled the great district of Strathnaver, which became known as Mackay country, and comprised the whole north-western corner of mainland Scotland.

Much of the land was sold in 1642, and the remainder of the Mackay country was sold to the house of Sutherland in 1829. Colonel Aeneas MacKay saw service in the Scots-Dutch Brigade in the 18th century, and his son was created a Baron of the Netherlands. This branch succeeded to the Barony of Reay.

57. MACKAY.

MacKenzie

BADGE: *Holly.*

MOTTO: *Luceo non uro (I shine, not burn).*

WAR CRY: *Tulach Ard! (A mountain in Kintail.)*

PIPE MUSIC: *Gairloch's lament.*

CLAIMING DESCENT from Colin, forefather of the Earls of the Ross who died in 1278, the MacKenzies held lands between Aird on the east coast and Kintail on the west coast, as well as the Isle of Lewis.

The western stronghold on Loch Diuch in Kintail was Eilan Donan Castle, perhaps the most picturesque of Scottish castles. Though this was sometimes held by their kin the Mathesons, it was usually held by the McRaes who became almost hereditary constables of the castle, and were known as 'Mackenzie's shirt of mail'. The family is famous in Canada for the explorer Sir Alexander MacKenzie (1764-1820) after whom MacKenzie river is named, and Alexander MacKenzie (1822-92) who was first Liberal prime minister of the then Dominion.

58. MACKENZIE

MacKinlay

THE ORIGINS of this clan are very obscure. It is thought that it may be descended through Drumnachill, a cadet of Buchanan, from Fionnladh MacArthur of that family.

59. MACKINLAY.

MacKinnon

BADGE: *Pine, St Columba's flower.*
MOTTO: *Audentes fortuna juvat (Fortune favours the bold).*
WAR CRY: *Cuimhnich bàs Ailpein!*

THE MACKINNONS seem to have belonged to the kindred of St Columba of Iona. MacKinnon means 'son of Fingon' and early references to the clan relate them to the island abbacy, though their original lands were in the north of neighbouring Mull. Though one of their plant badges, the pine, connects them to the clan Alpin, their chief badge is St Columba's flower. Iain MacKinnon, who died in 1500, was the last Abbot, whose tomb effigy is still to be seen at the renovated cathedral.

In the 14th century, the MacKinnons lost much of their land in Mull to the MacLeans, but at about this time they married into the MacLeods of Dunvegan and acquired extensive holdings in Skye.

60. MACKINNON.

MacLachlan

BADGE: *Mountain Ash or Periwinkle.*
MOTTO: *Fortis et fidus (Brave and trusty).*
PIPE MUSIC: *Moladh Mairi (In praise of Mary).*

THE GREAT CHIEF Lachlan Mor who lived by Loch Fyne in the 13th century was descended from Aodh O'Neill, son of the king of the North of Ireland (1030-33). The O'Neill ancestry can be traced back to pagan kings of Tara in the 4th century AD, and is considered to be the oldest traceable family left in Europe. The principal lands remain in Cowall and Knapdale in Argyllshire.

The Maclachlans were loyal Jacobites, and are said to have been with Bonnie Dundee at Killiecrankie in 1689, and in 1715 Lachlan MacLachlan of that Ilk signed the Address of welcome to the old Pretender. Colonel MacLachlan of that Ilk commanded a mixed regiment of MacLachlans and MacLeans at the Battle of Culloden, and was killed by a cannonball.

61. MACLACHLAN.

MacLaren

BADGE: *Laurel.*

MOTTO AND WAR CRY: *Creag an Tuirc*
(The Boar's rock).

THE CLAN MACLAREN lands were in Balquhidder which is in the highland part of Strathearn around Loch Voil and Loch Earn. Their ancestor was Laurence, Abbot of Balquihidder in the 13th century. They were so powerful and so numerous that it was said that no-one dared enter Balquhidder church until the MacLarens had taken their places. Though a warlike clan, they were twice overrun and massacred by the MacGregors, in 1542 and 1558. MacLarens saw service with the Kings of France and Sweden in the 15th and 16th centuries.

Loyal to the crown, the Maclarens fought for James III at Sauchieburn, James IV at Flodden, Queen Mary at Pinkie, and for Charles Edward at Culloden, where the clan suffered severely. MacLaren of Invernenty was taken prisoner after the battle, but in an incident described by Sir Walter Scott in *Redgauntlet*, he made his escape.

62. MACLAREN.

MacLean of Duart

BADGE: *Holly or crowberry.*
MOTTO: *Virtue mine honour.*
WAR CRIES: *Bas no beatta!*
    Fear eile airson Eachainn!
PIPE MUSIC: *The MacLean's Gathering.*

THIS POWERFUL and numerous clan has been seated in Mull from earliest times, but does not appear as an independent clan until the forfeiture of the Lord of the Isles in 1476. They are descended from Gilleain of the Battle Axe, whose lineage can be traced to the ancient Gaelic Kings of Dalriada.

For centuries, the MacLeans held the mighty Castle Duart on the Sound of Mull until they were evicted, some say swindled, out of their lands by the Campbells in the late 17th century. It was re-purchased in 1910 by Sir Fitzroy MacLean, the 19th Baronet. The war cry *'Fear eile airson Eachainn'* ('Another for Hector') stems from the battle of Inverlochy in 1632 when seven brothers of the clan died protecting their chief, Hector Reganach, with the cry on their lips. The Macleans were staunch Jacobites, rising in 1715 and 1745.

63. MACLEAN OF DUART

MacLaine
of Lochbuie

BADGE: *Crowberry*.
MOTTO: *Virtue mine honour*.
PIPE MUSIC: *Maclaine's march*.

THE BRANCH of MacLaines shares its ancestry
with the MacLeans of Duart, being descended
from Hector Reganach, brother of Lanclan Luba-
nach of the Duart branch. Which of the brothers
was the elder has never been established though the
Lochbuie clan claims seniority. The nominal lands
of the family were vast, including Lochiel, Duror,
Morven, Glencoe, Tiree, Jura, Scarba and Mull.
Though there was bitter rivalry between the two
branches of the family, they were reconciled after a
battle near Lochbuie when the Duart chief was
spared by the chief of Lochbuie.

As with the Duart branch, wild stories are told
of the Lochbuie MacLaines, including that of Ewen
MacLaine the younger, who was killed in battle
against his own father – Iain the Toothless. It is
said that when his ghost rides forth, it presages the
death of a MacLaine of Lochbuie.

64. MACLAINE OF LOCHBUIE.

MacLeod

BADGE: *Juniper or red whortleberry.*
MOTTO: *Hold fast.*
PIPE MUSIC: *MacLeod's praise, MacLeod's Lament.*

IN HIS BOOK *The Highland Clans*, Sir Iain Moncrieffe of that Ilk contends that the original Leod may have descended from the Norse kings of Man and the Hebrides. They 'sprang from the mighty Ynglingar royal stock whose ferocious royal ancestors are traced back in Sagas through king Halfdan the Stingy to Olaf Tree-Hewer (sacrificed to Woden by his own people during a time of famine)'. After the death of Magnus, the last king of Man in 1265, Lewis and Glenelg passed to the Macleods, acquiring vast tracts of Skye at about the same time.

Dunvegan Castle on Skye has been in the same family for the last seven centuries. Almost impregnable, it was about to be attacked by the celebrated Scots-American raider John Paul Jones in 1779, but mistaking a funeral procession for an armed body of clansmen, he hastened back to sea.

The MacLeods supported both Charles I and Charles II, but the famous ingratitude of those feckless monarchs caused the clan to refrain from joining in the Jacobite rebellions of the 18th century.

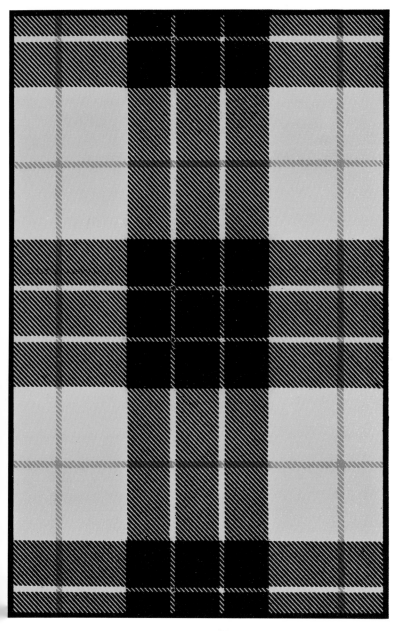

65. MACLEOD

MacMillan

BADGE: *Holly.*

MOTTO: *Misera succurrere disco (I learn to succour the distressed).*

IT SEEMS that the Macmillan surname is derived from the Gaelic *MacMhaolain* or 'son of the tonsured'. This implies descent from one of the old Celtic monastic houses. Many branches of the clan exist throughout Scotland, but the original lands were in Lochaber where the Macmillans were dependants of the clan Cameron. In the Middle Ages, the Macmillans acquired extensive lands in Knapdale through the heiress of the MacNeills. Through this connection, the coat of arms includes a royal lion.

The Macmillan tenure of Knapdale is commemorated by the beautiful Celtic carving on Macmillan's Cross.

66. MACMILLAN.

MacNab

BADGE: *Heath, pine, crowberry, bramble.*
MOTTO: *Timor omnis abesto (Let fear be far from all).*
PIPE MUSIC: *Macnab's Salute.*

THIS BRANCH of the great clan Alpine is of ecclesiastical origin, MacNab meaning son of the Abbot. Indeed, they are descended from the Celtic hereditary Abbots of Glendochart. In the 13th century the Abbot still ranked with the Earl's of Atholl and Monteith, but because the MacNabs sided with the Macdougalls against Robert the Bruce, they lost most of their possessions after Bannockburn, retaining only the Barony of Bovain.

The MacNabs supported the Stuarts during the Civil Wars, and in the 1745 rising, the chief supported the government but the clan sided with Charles Edward. In 1828, an old prophesy was fulfilled, that 'when a great storm blew a branch of a pine tree against the trunk of another, and grafted itself into the trunk, the MacNabs would lose their lands' and the old clan lands were sold to pay debts. In 1929, the 22nd chief bought back 7000 acres of the clan country.

67. MACNAB.

MacNaughton

BADGE: *Trailing azalea.*
MOTTO: *I hope in God.*
WAR CRY: *Fraoch-Eilean!*

THE CLAN of the sons of Nachtan claims Pictish descent from the royal house of Lorn in the Dark ages. It first came to prominence in the 12th century, and in the 13th Gillechrist MacNaughton received from Alexander III a charter of hereditary keepership of the royal castle of Fraoch Eilean, the heathery isle in Loch Awe. Their lands bordered Loch Awe and Loch Fyne, but their opposition to Robert the Bruce resulted in the forfeiture of most of the lands.

The chief of the clan, Alexander, was knighted by James IV, but was killed at the Battle of Flodden in 1513. The clan was loyal to the Stuart cause, and another chief Alexander was knighted by Charles II after the Restoration. The remaining lands were forfeited to the Crown after the Battle of Killie-crankie, and the senior branch emigrated to Antrim in Ireland in the 18th century.

68. MACNAUGHTON.

MacNeil

BADGE: *Dryas*.

MOTTO: *Vincere vel mori*
  (To conquer or die).

WAR CRY: *Buaidh no bàs!*

PIPE MUSIC: *MacNeil of Barra's March*.

THE MACNEILS are descended from the old High Kings of Ireland through Aodh O'Neill, king of the North of Ireland (1030-33). The clan is divided into the MacNeils of Barr and the MacNeils of Gigha, and the former branch is acknowledged as the senior. Originally the clan held the island of Gigha and lands in Knapdale, and were hereditary keepers of Castle Swin; from this branch the MacNeils of Colonsay descended. The possessions in the Outer Hebrides, Barra and Boisdale in South Uist principally, seem to have been acquired in the 14th century.

The MacNeils were staunch Jacobites, but their very remoteness made participation in the 1715 and 1745 tangential at best. Many of the MacNeils of Barra emigrated to North America, and the chieftainship emigrated with them. In 1937 Robert MacNeil returned from America and recovered much of Barra and the historic Kisimul Castle which he restored.

69. MACNEIL.

MacPherson

BADGE: *Box, white heather*.
MOTTO: *Touch not the cat bott a glove*.
WAR CRY: *Creag Dhubh Chloinn Chatain!*
PIPE MUSIC: *MacPherson's March*.

THE CLAN MacPherson has many branches, but the principal one, the Macphersons of Cluny, are descended from Duncan the parson, who, as hereditary lay parson of Kingussie, flourished in the mid 15th century. The clan is a member of the great clan Chattan confederation, and enjoys close links with the clan Mackintosh. The Macphersons first appear in Badenoch in the 16th century, and came to hold the great mountainous district from Kingussie to Ben Alder and Loch Laggan with a long stretch of the Spey.

The MacPhersons were loyal to the Stuart cause in 1640, and again in the Risings of 1715 and 1745. The clan took part in several engagements of the 1745 Rising, but arrived too late to fight at Culloden. However, MacPherson of Cluny actively assisted Charles Edward in his escape, and for nine years evaded capture, loyally protected by his clansmen in spite of a reward of £1000 being offered for his capture.

70. MACPHERSON, DRESS.

Hunting MacPherson

THIS PATTERN is said to have been made for Janet, daughter of Simon, 11th Lord Fraser of Lovat, and wife of Ewen MacPherson, from an old plaid which was preserved in Cluny Castle for generations.

71. MACPHERSON, HUNTING.

MacQuarrie

BADGE: *Pine*.

MOTTO AND WAR CRY: *An t'Arm
    breac dearg*.

PIPE MUSIC: *The red tartaned army*.

THE MACQUARRIES are members of the great clan Alpine, and are said to be descended through the female line from St. Columba. This extends their ancestry back to the High kings of Ireland who were reigning in Tara when the Roman legions left Britain. The traditional home of the MacQuarries was the Isle of Ulva off the west coast of Mull, and they followed the Lord of the Isles until the title was extinguished, and then the MacLeans of Duart.

The last known chief of the MacQuarries entertained Dr Johnson and James Boswell, but was forced to sell his lands in 1778, dying on Mull aged 103 in 1818. A kinsman, General Lachlan MacQuarrie, succeeded the notorious Captain Bligh as Governor of New South Wales, and the Lachlan and MacQuarrie rivers are named after him.

72. MACQUARRIE.

MacRae

BADGE: *Club moss.*
MOTTO: *Fortitudine (With fortitude).*
WAR CRY: *Sgur urain!*
PIPE MUSIC: *MacRae's March.*

THE NAME MACRAE, meaning son of grace, is thought to be of ecclesiastical origin. The clan originated in Beauly in Invernesshire, but removed to Kintail on the west coast of Scotland in the 14th century.

The MacRaes were loyal followers of the Mac-Kenzies, Lord of Kintail and Earls of Seaforth, and the clan beame known as 'Mackenzie's Shirt of Mail.' The MacRaes became constables of the Mackenzies' chief stronghold, Eilean Donan Castle on Loch Duich, and also Chamberlains of Kintail. The clan did not rise for Charles Edward in 1745, but many individual members took part in the Rising.

78. MACRAE.

MacQueen

BADGE: *Box.*
MOTTO: *Constant and faithful.*

RODERICK MACSWEYN or MacQueen is said to be the founder of this clan in the 15th century, though the MacSweens first appear in the 13th century as keepers of Castle Sween in Kintyre. As a distinct clan they are first noted as fighting under the banner of MacIntosh, captain of the clan Chattan at the Battle of Harlaw in 1411.

The MacQueens settled in Strathdearn, and by the 16th century they were holding the lands of Corrybrough. The lands passed out of the family in the 18th century.

74. MACQUEEN.

Malcolm

BADGE: *Mountain ash.*

MOTTO: *In ardua tendit (He aims at difficult things).*

THE MALCOLMS or Macallums (sons of Columba) take their name from the Gaelic *Maol Chaluim*. They owed their allegiance to the Campbells, and in 1414 the Cambell chief made Ronald MacCallum of Corbarron the hereditary Constable of Craignish Castle.

The name was Englished by Alexander Malcolm, 9th of Portalloch (acquired in 1562) in the 18th century. By intermarriage with the Campbells, the family became proprietors of Duntrune Castle, still owned by the Malcolm family. John Malcolm, 17th of Poltalloch, married the daughter of the famous Edwardian beauty Lily Langtry, the 'Jersey lily'.

75. MALCOLM.

Matheson

BADGE: *Broom.*
MOTTO: *Fac et spera (Do and hope).*
WAR CRY: *Dail Achadh'n da thearnaidh!*

MATHESON derives from the Gaelic *Mac-Mhathain* meaning 'Sun of the bear' and the clan is of the same group as the MacKenzies. They supported the Earls of Ross, and Cormas, the second Matheson chief, was rewarded in 1264 for help in campaigns against the Norsemen. By the early 15th century the Mathesons could raise an army of 2000 men.

The clan is divided into two main branches, those of Lochalsh and those of Shiness in Sutherland. Both branches produced remarkable men of fortune. James Sutherland Matheson, of the Shiness family, born in 1796, was a founder of the mighty Hong Kong trading firm Jardine Matheson and Co, and purchased the Isle of Lewis in 1844. Alexander Matheson of the Lochalsh family, born in 1805, also made a fortune in the East, and spent over £1 million buying and improving 220,000 acres in Ross-shire.

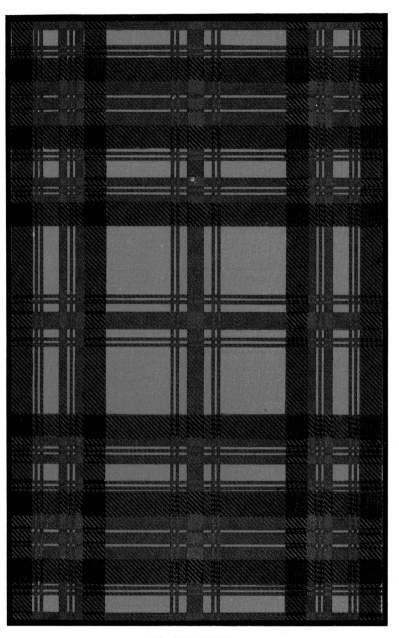

76. MATHESON.

Maxwell

BADGE: *A stag before a holly bush.*
MOTTO: *Reviresco (I flourish again).*

THIS POWERFUL Border family takes its name from the parish of Maxwell on the river Tweed near Kelso. 'Macca's Well' is named after Maccus, the 11th century king of Man. The two chief branches of the family are descended from Herbert Maxwell and John Maxwell, sons of Sir Aymer Maxwell whose brother had been Chamberlain of Scotland.

The Maxwells seem to have been typical of the Marcher lords made familiar in traditional ballad and later romances, such as Sir Walter Scott's *Marmion*. John, 3rd Lord Maxwell, was killed at Flodden. A feud with the Johnstons resulted in the murder of Sir James Johnston in 1608 and the execution of the 7th Lord, John Maxwell for this killing in 1613. His brother was made Earl of Nithsdale, but the 5th Earl came out for the Old Pretender in 1715 and was condemned to death. Whilst awaiting execution in the Tower of London, his wife helped him escape dressed as a woman.

77. MAXWELL.

Menzies

BADGE: *The Menzies heath.*
MOTTO: *Vill God I Zall*
(Will God I shall).
WAR CRY: *Gael' us Dearg a suas!*
PIPE MUSIC: *Menzies March.*

THE SURNAME of Menzies is of Anglo-Norman derivation, from Mesnieres, near Rouen in Normandy. It shares this root with the English family name Manners, who became Dukes of Rutland. The first Menzies (pronounced Mingies) of note in Scottish history was Robert de Menyers who was Lord High Chamberlain in the mid 13th century. The traditional Menzies lands were Weem, Aberfeldy and Glendochart in Perthshire.

The Menzies supported Bruce at Bannockburn, and ninety years later we find David Menzies Governor of Orkney and Shetland under the King of Norway. A later distinction of the family is botanical; in 1738 Menzies of Culdares brought back from the Tyrol the first larches to be introduced to Scotland. It is said that two large trees in the Dunkeld grounds of the Duke of Atholl are grown from the saplings brought back in Menzies' portmanteau. The tinctures of the Menzies arms are invoked in the battle cry, which means 'Up with the White and Red!'

168

78. MENZIES.

Munro

BADGE: *Club moss.*
MOTTO: *Dread God.*
WAR CRY: *Caistel Foulis'n a Theine!*
PIPE MUSIC: *Munro's March.*

THE GAELIC clan name was *Rothach*, or 'men of Ro'. The place-name is unidentified but the Munro seem to have always been in Easter Ross and the lands to the north of the Cromarty Firth. The title of the chief was and is Munro of Foulis, a castle between Dingwall and Invergordon, on whose highest tower a beacon was lit as a rallying signal in times of clan warfare.

The Munros were loyal supporters of the Earls of Ross, and from earliest times seem to have been skilled and valiant soldiers. Many served under Gustavus Adolphus; at one stage there were 27 Field Officers and 11 captains all bearing the name Munro serving in the Swedish army. Sir Robert Munro commanded the Black Watch at Fontenoy and was killed at Falkirk, fighting off half-a-dozen Camerons before being shot by a seventh. James Monroe twice president of the United States and author of the Monroe Doctrine is probably descended from the medieval Monro chiefs of Foulis.

79. MUNRO.

Murray
of Atholl

BADGE: *Butchers Broom*
MOTTO: *Tout Pret (Quite ready)*.
PIPE MUSIC: *Atholl highlander*.

MURRAY COMES FROM the great province of
Moray – *Moireabh* in Gaelic, *Moravia* in Latin.
This large clan had branches scattered throughout
Scotland from Sutherland, where the Earls were
Murrays to the Borders. Through marriage, Sir
Walter Murray was 1st Lord of Bothwell in
Clydesdale in the mid 13th century, but this line
died out, the widow of the last Murray of Bothwell
remarrying the 3rd Earl of Douglas. By the
sixteenth century, the headship of the clan was
recognised to be Murray of Tullibardine in
Strathearn.

In 1629 John Murray obtained the title of Earl
of Atholl, and his son John married Lady Amelia
Stanley, daughter of the Earl of Derby, through
whom he acquired lordship of the Isle of Man. He
was created Marquis of Atholl, and his son John, a
strong supporter of William III, was created Duke
in 1703. The Duke of Atholl commands the Atholl
Highlanders, the only private bodyguard in the
realm. Their principal duties are to guard Royal
visitors to Blair Castle. Among the most notable
members of this distinguished family can be numbered Lord George Murray, the brilliant and
honourable Jacobite general, and the great lawyer
William Murray, first Earl of Mansfield.

80. MURRAY OF ATHOLE.

The Clan of Murray

BADGE: *Butchers Broom or juniper.*
MOTTO: *Tout Pret (Quite ready).*

THIS TARTAN, sometimes erroneously called Tullibardine, was adopted and worn by Charles, first Earl of Dunmore, himself the second son of the first Marquis of Atholl and his wife Lady Amelia Stanley, by whom the sovereignty of the Isle of Man and the Barony of Strange came into the family. He was thus sixth in descent from Mary, Queen Dowager of France, the beautiful daughter of King Henry VII through the Stanleys, Earls of Derby, and the Cliffords, Earls of Cumberland.

81. MURRAY OF TULLIBARDINE.

Ogilvie

BADGE: *Evergreen alkanet, whitethorn, hawthorn.*

MOTTO: *A fin (To the end).*

THE OGILVIES are descended from the ancient Kings of Angus, who after the union of the Picts and the Gaels became Earls of Angus and were one of the 'seven Earls of Scotland' who were peers of the King of the Scots. The present clan can be traced back to Gilbert, younger son of the Earl of Angus, who was given the lands of Ogilvie in Angus in the 12th century. In the 15th century, Sir Walter Ogilvie built the Tower of Airlie (burnt by the Campbells in 1640) and Sir James Ogilvie was created Lord Ogilvie of Airlie in 1491.

For his devotion to Charles I, James, 8th Lord Ogilvie was created Earl of Airlie. David Ogilvie, son of the 4th Earl, joined the Stuart cause in 1745, was attainted and fled to France, and became an officer in the French service. It is said that whenever the Earl of Airlie is about to die, the spirit of a drummer boy may be heard beating his ghostly drum. This warning was last heard in 1900 by Lady Airlie. Unbeknown to her, her husband the 8th Earl was leading a cavalry charge at the Battle of Diamond Hill in South Africa in which he was killed.

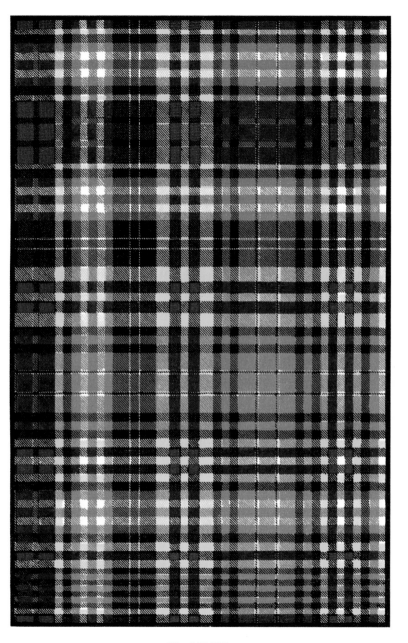

82. OGILVIE.

Robertson

BADGE: *Fine leaved heath or fern.*
MOTTO: *Virtutis gloria marces*
    (Glory is the reward of valour).
WAR CRY: *Gargn uair dhuis gear!*
PIPE MUSIC: *The Robertsons have come.*

THE ROBERTSONS of Struan are one of the oldest Scottish families, descended through the Celtic Earls of Atholl from the family of St. Columba. They take their name from Robert Riach (Grizzled Robert) of the clan Donnachaidh. His lands were designated the Barony of Struan in 1451 by King James II as a reward for the capture of Sir Robert Graham, who had murdered James I in 1437.

Duncan Robertson, the Fat, was a loyal supporter of Bruce, and his descendants adhered closely to the Jacobite cause. The remarkable chief Alexander was a poet of some note, and supported Dundee in 1688 and was attainted. His attainter having been remitted, he was out again for the Old Pretender in 1715, captured at Sheriffmuir, escaped to France, and was pardoned in 1731. He joined Charles Edward in 1745 but was too old to fight and returned home, dying in 1749. The Reids are also descended from Donnachaidh, and sometimes style themselves Robertson.

83. ROBERTSON.

The Rob Roy Tartan

BECAUSE OF BRIGANDAGE and lawlessness, the use of the name MacGregor was proscribed in 1603, and it is thought that the most notorious of the clan, Rob Roy Campbell MacGregor, adopted this simple tartan in lieu of the clan sett.

Rob Roy was a gentleman drover, and after the death of his father he was tutor to and manager of the properties of his nephew, MacGregor of Glenlyon. However, a dispute with the Duke of Montrose caused him to take refuge in the mountains, raiding the Dukes estates continuously, and by 1712 he had a price on his head. He remained a brigand in outlook and even though he came out for the Old pretender in 1715, commanding a force of MacGregors, at the battle of Sheriffmuir he did not advance against the enemy, but contented himself by raiding the baggage trains of friend and foe alike.

He was by no means the romantic hero described by Sir Walter Scott, but he was an excellent swordsman and able commander. He captured the government fort at Inversnaid, torched it and dispersed the garrison. He died in 1734 aged about seventy.

84. ROB ROY.

Rose

BADGE: *Wild rosemary.*
MOTTO: *Constant and true.*

THE ROSES OF KILRAVOCK have enjoyed their property through over twenty generations. The Roses seem to be descended from the Norman de Rose, and the family was in Scotland as early as the reign of David I in the 12th Century. However, documentary evidence of the Kilravock family begins in the reign of Alexander II (1198-1249), at which time they held the lands of Geddes in Inverness-shire. The barony of Kilravock passed into the family by marriage, and the deed of conveyance was confirmed by a charter from John Balliol in 1293. A charter securing all the Rose lands was procured *de novo* in the 15th century as a provision against adverse claims in those troubled times.

Hugh Rose built the old tower of Kilravock on the river Nairn in 1460, and the Barons of Kilravock intermarried with many of the prominent families of the north and filled various situations of high trust and honour.

85. ROSE.

Ross

BADGE: *Juniper.*
MOTTO: *Spem successus alit (Success nourishes hope).*
PIPE MUSIC: *The Earl of Ross's March.*

THE CLAN OF ROSS take their name from the province of Ross, and are descended from Ferchar, the first Earl of Ross. He was Ferchar *Macc in t'Sagairt* (son of the priest) who held the vast district of Applecross in Wester Ross by inheritance from the O'Beotain hereditary abbots of Applecross. It is likely that this family is of Irish stock, related to the O'Beolain hereditary abbots of Drumcliff. The 3rd Earl led the clan at the battle of Bannockburn and the 5th Earl was killed at the battle of Halidon Hill in 1333. The 6th Earl died without issue, after a struggle for the earldom between the Lord of the Isles and the Regent Albany, it reverted to the crown in 1424.

The chieftainship of the clan passed to the Rosses of Balnagowan, who held it for over three centuries. The Balnagowan estates went to the Lockhart family, who assumed the name of Ross in the 18th century. Colonel George Ross, descended from the Rosses of Balnagowan, was one of the signatories of the American Declaration of Independence.

86. ROSS.

Scott

BADGE: *A golden stag.*
MOTTO: *Amo (I love).*
WAR CRY: *A Bellandean!*

T HE SCOTTS take their name from the Latin
appellation of the Irish tribe which gave its
name to Scotland. Uchtredus filius Scoti, the
forbear of the two principal Scott lines of Buccleuch
and Balweary, lived in the early 12th century. The
Buccleuch branch of this powerful Border family
was ennobled by James VI, and on the failure of
the male line the countess of Buccleuch married the
Duke of Monmouth, bastard of Charles II, who
was created Duke of Buccleuch. Their grandson,
the 3rd Duke, succeeded to the Dukedom of
Queensberry.

The Scotts of Balweary, now represented by the
Scotts of Ancrum, acquired their lands by marriage.
The most notable member of this branch was the
great scholar and translator Sir Michael Scott
(c.1175-1234) who learned Arabic at Toledo and
was the author of several astrological and occult
works. He was credited with magical exploits, and
in popular legend the possessor of a demon horse
and a demon ship. The celebrated novelist and poet
Sir Walter Scott was descended from the cadet
branch of the Scotts of Harden.

87. SCOTT.

Sinclair

BADGE: *Whin or gorse.*
MOTTO: *Commit thy work to God.*
PIPE MUSIC: *The Sinclair's March.*

THE COLOURFUL SINCLAIR family is descended from William, son of the Comte de Saint Clair in Normandy, who came to England with William the Conqueror. He settled in Scotland, and his descendants were granted the barony of Roslin in MidLothian in the 12th century. Sir William Sinclair accompanied Sir James Douglas to Spain with the heart of Robert the Bruce, and was killed fighting the Moors. His son Henry acquired the Earldom of Orkney in 1379 and the 3rd Earl received the Earldom of Caithness in 1455. The Earls of Caithness and the Viscounts Thurso are descended from this family.

In 1391 Henry, Earl of Orkney, enlisted a ship-wrecked Venetian to captain a fleet of exploration. There is good evidence that the expedition reached Nova Scotia, and an effigy in Massachussets is thought to record the event. The stronghold of the Sinclairs was firstly the Castle of Mey (since owned by Queen Elizabeth the Queen Mother) and Girnigoe Castle, now ruined, where George Sinclair, 4th Earl of Caithness, imprisoned his eldest son. On being taunted in his cell by his younger brother, the Master of Caithness attacked him with his chain causing his death some days later, but the Master, in turn, was starved to death in prison.

88. SINCLAIR.

Skene

BADGE: *An arm holding a laurel wreath.*
MOTTO: *Virtutis regia merces (A palace
is the reward of bravery).*

TRADITION ASSERTS that the Skenes are descended from the Robertsons of Struan, and
that the first of them was so called for having killed
with only his skene (or dagger) an enormous wolf
which endangered the life of Malcolm III. The king
offered him the choice of as much land as a hound
could course around or hawk could cover in flight.
He chose the latter, and received the lands of Skene
in Aberdeenshire between the rivers Dee and Don.
Robert de Skene was a faithful follower of Robert
the Bruce, and he received from the king a charter
erecting the lands of Skene into a barony.

Three Skene chiefs died in battle: Adam de Skene
at Harlaw in 1411, Alexander Skene of that Ilk at
Flodden in 1513, and his grandson Alexander at
Pinkie in 1547. In 1827, the last Skene of that Ilk
died without issue, and the estates passed to his
nephew, the Earl of Fife, whose mother was Mary,
daughter of George Skene of Skene.

89. SKENE.

Old Stewart

BADGE: *Oak, thistle.*

MOTTO: *Virescit vulnere virtus (Courage grows strong at a wound).*

WAR CRY: *Creag-an-Sgairbh!*

PIPE MUSIC: *The Stewart's White Banner. My king has landed in Moidart.*

THIS TARTAN has been known for two hundred years as 'the Stewart Tartan' and is supposed to have been worn in former times by such families as the Stewarts of Appin and the Stewarts of Grandtully.

90. OLD STEWART.

Royal Stewart

BADGE: *Oak, thistle.*

MOTTO: *Virescit vulnere virtus (Courage grows strong at a wound).*

WAR CRY: *Creag-an-sgairbh!*

PIPE MUSIC: *The Stewart's white Banner. My king has landed in Moidart.*

WALTER, THE SON of an Anglo-Norman baron, Alan, Lord of Oswestry, was appointed high Steward of the royal household by David I. The office was made hereditary by Malcolm IV, and the fifth High Steward was a staunch supporter of William Wallace and Robert the Bruce in their struggle for Scottish independence. His son Walter, 6th high Steward, married Robert the Bruce's daughter Marjory, and from them are descended the Royal House of Stewart. The male line of the Stewarts (or Stuarts) ended in 1807 with the death of Henry, Cardinal Duke of York. He was the second son of the Old Pretender, and was at Dunkirk at the head of 15,000 French troops assembled to assist Prince Charles Edward when the fatal news of Culloden arrived. Thereafter he exchanged his sword for the cowl.

In Scotland, the first four dukes and the first marquis ever to be created were all Stewarts, and at one time or another the family has held seventeen earldoms.

The Royal Stewart tartan is regarded as the personal tartan at the Royal House of Scotland, and is considered to be the Royal tartan of H.M. The Queen.

91. STEWART, ROYAL.

Hunting Stewart

BADGE: *Thistle*.

THE ORIGIN OF THIS handsome tartan is obscure. Its predominently dark colours are typical of hunting setts where concealment in rocks and heather is the main consideration.

92. STEWART HUNTING

Dress Stewart

BADGE: *Oak.*

DRESS TARTANS have a white background and are variations of the clan pattern. They were originally worn by the ladies of a clan, and this old dress tartan of the Royal Stewarts was revived by Queen Victoria, for which reason it is sometimes known as the Victoria Tartan.

93. STEWART, DRESS.

Prince Charles Stewart

BADGE: *Oak*.

THIS TARTAN, which is associated with the memory of that hapless Prince, is the same as the Royal Stewart (or Stuart) tartan, except that the broad red stripe is very much contracted.

Charles Edward died in the arms of the Master of Nairn in Frascati in 1788. His body was later removed to St Peter's, Rome, where a monument, the work of Canova, was erected to him, his father and his brother, by the desire of King George IV.

94. STEWART, PRINCE CHARLES EDWARD.

Sutherland

BADGE: *Butcher's Broom or Cotton-sedge*.
MOTTO: *Sans peur (Without fear)*.
WAR CRY: *Ceann na drochaide bige!*
PIPE MUSIC: *The Sutherlands*.

THE SUTHERLAND CLAN take their name from the highlands of the far north of Scotland which is known as 'Sutherland' because to the Norsemen it was the *Sudr-land* that lay to the south of their settlements in Orkney and Caithness. The Sutherlands are descended from Freskin, a Flemish noble who had married into the Picto-Scottish royal house of Moray. Their immediate forbear was Hugh de Moray who was granted the lands by William the Lion. His son William was created Earl of Sutherland in about 1230, and it is claimed to be the oldest earldom in Britain.

In the 16th century the earldom passed to Adam Gordon of Aboyne, and the last Gordon earl died in 1766 without male issue. His daughter Elizabeth, countess of Sutherland, married George Granville Leveson-Gower, later Marquis of Stafford, who was created Duke of Sutherland in 1833.

95. SUTHERLAND.

Urquhart

BADGE: *Wallflower, gillyflower.*
MOTTO: *Mean, speak and do weil.*

TRADITION HAS IT that the Urquhart family is closely connected with the original Forbes chiefs. They take their name from 'the fort on the Knoll', the mighty Castle Urquhart on Loch Ness, from which control of the north-eastern end of the Great Glen was exercised in medieval times. The constable of Castle Urquhart was usually Sheriff of Inverness. William of Urquhart, who had married a daughter of the Earl of Ross, became Sheriff of Cromarty in the reign of Robert the Bruce, and his son Adam was granted the same Sheriffdom in 1258, which thereafter became hereditary.

The chief of the Urquhart clan is an American citizen. Perhaps his most notable forbear was Thomas Urquhart of Cromarty, knighted by Charles I. He translated Rabelais into English, traced his lineage from Adam and Eve (143rd generation in direct descent), nearly destroyed the castle of Inverness in 1649, and is said to have died from a fit of joyful laughter on hearing of the restoration of Charles II to the throne.

96. URQUHART